PowerKiDS Readers
SAFARI ANIMALS

ZEBRAS

Clara Reade

PowerKiDS press.
New York

For Henry Chesnut

Published in 2013 by The Rosen Publishing Group, Inc.
29 East 21st Street, New York, NY 10010

First Edition

Editor: Amelie von Zumbusch
Book Design: Greg Tucker

Photo Credits: Cover, pp. 5, 7, 9, 11, 13, 15, 17, 19, 21, 23, 24 Shutterstock.com.

Library of Congress Cataloging-in-Publication Data

Reade, Clara.
Zebras / by Clara Reade. — 1st ed.
p. cm. — (Powerkids readers: safari animals)
Includes index.
ISBN 978-1-4488-7395-1 (library binding) — ISBN 978-1-4488-7535-1 (pbk.) —
ISBN 978-1-4488-7548-1 (6-pack)
1. Zebras—Juvenile literature. I. Title.
QL737.U62R43 2013
599.665'7—dc23
2011050660

Manufactured in the United States of America

CPSIA Compliance Information: Batch #CS12PK: For Further Information contact Rosen Publishing, New York, New York at 1-800-237-9932

CONTENTS

Zebras are in the horse family.

They run fast.

Grass is their main food.

They sleep standing up.

Zebras live in Africa.

They have striped **coats**.

The skin under their coats is black.

Each zebra's stripes
are different.

Baby zebras are **foals**.

Foals can run an hour after they are born.

WORDS TO KNOW

coat

foal

zebra

INDEX

WEBSITES

Due to the changing nature of Internet links, PowerKids Press has developed an online list of websites related to the subject of this book. This site is updated regularly. Please use this link to access the list:
www.powerkidslinks.com/pkrs/zeb/